BOOKWORMS

Nature's Formations

How Are Caves Formed?

B.J. Best

Cavendish Square
New York

Published in 2018 by Cavendish Square Publishing, LLC
243 5th Avenue, Suite 136, New York, NY 10016

First Edition

CPSIA Compliance Information: Batch #CS17CSQ

All websites were available and accurate when this book was sent to press.

Library of Congress Cataloging-in-Publication Data

Names: Best, B. J., 1976-
Title: How are caves formed? / B.J. Best.
Description: New York : Cavendish Square Publishing, [2018] | Series: Nature's formations | Includes index.
Identifiers: LCCN 2016046832 (print) | LCCN 2016047318 (ebook) | ISBN 9781502625366 (pbk.) |ISBN 9781502625335 (6 pack) | ISBN 9781502625342 (library bound) | ISBN 9781502625359 (E-book)
Subjects: LCSH: Caves--Juvenile literature.
Classification: LCC GB601.2 .B47 2017 (print) | LCC GB601.2 (ebook) | DDC 551.44/7--dc23
LC record available at https://lccn.loc.gov/2016046832

Editorial Director: David McNamara
Copy Editor: Nathan Heidelberger
Associate Art Director: Amy Greenan
Designer: Alan Sliwinski
Production Assistant: Karol Szymczuk
Photo Research: J8 Media

The photographs in this book are used by permission and through the courtesy of: Photo credits: Cover Aleksander Rubtsova/Getty Images; p. 5 Doug Meek/Shutterstock.com; p. 7 Studio2013/Shutterstock.com; p. 10 Mangojuicy/Shutterstock.com; p. 11 Imagentle/ Shutterstock.com; p. 13 Pavelk/Shutterstock.com; p. 15 MyImages/Micha/Shutterstock.com; p. 17 Joshua Haviv/Shutterstock.com; p. 19 Outcast85/Shutterstock.com; p. 21 Chris Howes/Wild Places Photography/Alamy Stock Photo.

Printed in the United States of America

Contents

Caves are tunnels underground.

Some are small.

Some are huge!

There is solid rock under dirt and soil.

This is called **bedrock**.

Most caves are made from **limestone** bedrock.

This stone can have cracks in it.

Caves are made by water.

Rain falls through the air.

It becomes a gentle **acid**.

This acid sinks through the soil.

It hits the bedrock.

The acid enters the cracks in the rock.

It slowly eats the rock away.

It can take many thousands of years to make a cave.

Sometimes it takes millions of years!

Caves can be wet.

The water is still **shaping** the cave.

Cave exploring is called **spelunking**.

People love seeing the strange rocks of caves!

New Words

acid (AA-sid) A liquid that breaks down something.

bedrock (BED-rock) Solid rock under soil.

limestone (LIME-stone) Rock where caves are formed.

shaping (SHAYP-ing) Changing the shape of something.

spelunking (speh-LUHNK-ing) Cave exploring.

Index

About the Author

B.J. Best lives in Wisconsin with his wife and son. He has written many other books for children. His favorite cave is Wind Cave in South Dakota.

About BOOKWORMS

Bookworms help independent readers gain reading confidence through high-frequency words, simple sentences, and strong picture/text support. Each book explores a concept that helps children relate what they read to the world they live in.